Grandma's Tears

Grandma's Tears

Comfort for Grieving Grandparents

June Cerza Kolf

Baker Books

A Division of Baker Book House Co
Grand Rapids, Michigan 49516

©1995 by June Cerza Kolf

Published by Baker Books
a division of Baker Book House Company
P.O. Box 6287, Grand Rapids, MI 49516-6287

Printed in the United States of America

Library of Congress Cataloging-in-Publication Data

Kolf, June Cerza
    Grandma's tears : comfort for grieving grandparents /
by June Cerza Kolf.
    p.   cm.
    Includes bibliographical references.
    ISBN 0-8010-5264-5
    1. Bereavement—Psychological aspects. 2. Grief. 3.
Death—Psychological aspects. 4. Grandparents. 5. Grandparents and child. I. Title.
BF575.G7K634   1995
155.9'37—dc20   94-40866

Written especially for
Annie Christensen,
a very special grandma
and the most loving person I know.
I wanted to take her home with me
and keep her,
but her family wouldn't allow it.

*My heart aches for my child
without a child.*

—Cheral Hymen,
grandmother of
two "Distant Angels"

Contents

Acknowledgments

At the completion of this book, before it went to press, my eighty-seven-year-old mother became critically ill. Although I was given the precious gift of a final visit with her, I was not present at the time of her death.

I want to thank the two very special ladies who gently eased her home: my sister by birth, Barbara Grek, and my sister through marriage, Beverly Cerza.

I love you both.

Introduction

everal years ago, when my daughter was expecting her first baby (my first grandchild), a book title, *Grandma's Tears*, flashed across my mind. Because I was afraid of the pain I would have to endure in order to write a book with that title, I sent it away as quickly as it appeared.

Fortunately, however, my role as a grandparent brought me great joy. So I was somewhat puzzled over the title *Grandma's Tears* that continued to flit in and out of the creative corners of my mind.

A few months ago an event took place that solved the puzzle of the mysterious title that was hovering around me. I was leading a grief support group, as I have been doing for the past ten years. Although each group takes on a character of its own, this particular group was an unusual mix. I struggled to find the right words to soothe the hearts of parents, two grandmothers, a granddaughter, a sibling, and a wife all at the same time.

We had been meeting for several weeks and I had become well acquainted with a couple who were grieving the loss of their son. The boy's grandmother, who was visiting from out of town, attended the meetings with them as they all struggled to adjust to their devastating loss. Each week as the parents poured out their pain, the grandmother patted them lovingly while she daintily dabbed at her own eyes.

I thought about how wonderful it was that she was able to be with them and how blessed they were to have her to lean on in their time of need. It reinforced my awareness of the importance of loving families in desperate situations. However, the evening the grandmother spoke to us directly from her heart, my eyes were opened in an entirely different way.

As I listened to her words, I realized that her loss was like none other that I had seen. She was truly one of the *forgotten grievers*. When a child dies we all grieve for the parents, but we often forget about the grandparents. We forget that they, too, are trying to survive, often with little or no support of their own.

Annie had suffered the death of her grandson and, as a grandmother myself, I know that the love felt for a grandchild is unlike any other. It is a pure and unselfish love that makes your heart feel perpetually like the first time you fell in love. It is endless, irrational, and oftentimes ridiculous. But, most of all, it is something that can only be understood by another grandparent.

When Annie lost her grandson, she suffered a heartwrenching wound, but in addition to her own pain, she had to watch the pain of her daughter and son-in-law in their roles as grieving parents. As much as she wanted to comfort them, there was no way she could bring back their son. All of this resulted in a double whammy. The pain multiplied each day as she endured her own grief and had to watch helplessly as her children suffered their personal loss.

While I was listening to Annie speak, *Grandma's Tears* crept out of the recesses of my mind. Only this time it didn't return to its hiding place. It became the title of this book written for that very special group of people—grieving grandparents.

I pray that grieving grandparents who read this book will know that they are not alone in their suffering and that the pain they are experiencing is normal. By applying the three powerful T's—time, talk, and tears—they, too, will someday heal.

The Needs

he sound of the ringing telephone shat-tered the stillness of the night. I reached my hand out from under the warmth of the blankets to pick up the phone. I had no idea that my life was about to be changed forever with that one sim-ple gesture.

Mary was remembering the night she received the news that her grandson had been in a car accident.

In a split second the news of the death of a loved one alters our lives irreversibly. We will never again be exactly who we were before receiving the news. Each death we experience in our lives will affect us differently. Some will be easier to adjust to than others, but they will all change us so that we will never be the same again.

17

The death of a grandchild is a loss like no other. Upon hearing the news, you are stunned and speechless. When you try to find the words to console other family members, nothing seems to come out right. The words seem trite and insignificant. You choke on the lump in your throat and begin to cry, feeling as if you are only making matters more difficult. You want to offer suggestions, but at the same time you don't want to impose or seem to be taking charge. The balance is delicate.

You will want to grab your grown child, who is now grieving the loss of his or her own child, and kiss away the hurt. You may want to say that everything will be all right like you used to do when he or she was a young child. Yet there is no bandage to place on this wound, so you feel more helpless than ever before in your life.

During all of this, your own heart is being shattered into a million pieces as you think about your beloved grandchild who will never again sit at your dinner table or cuddle next to you on the couch.

Because you are one of the older generation you may feel you should have all the right answers or a secret formula to ease everyone else's pain. However, it is not possible for one individual to have all the answers. Forgive yourself for not knowing what to say or for not having perfect words of comfort to offer. You are hurting too, and to lay guilt on yourself at this time is fruitless.

If the death occurred suddenly, there will be great confusion as long lists of decisions have to be made. People who are grieving often have short tempers and lash out at those closest to them. If your grieving child lashes out at you, do not take it personally. Be ready to forgive, and understand that the anger directed toward you is the result of the loss and not a lack of love on your child's part.

Prayerfully participate in decision-making when you are asked, but do not feel excluded if you happen to be overlooked. Shock and confusion can cause strange reactions, and sometimes grandparents must wait on the sidelines until things settle down a little.

The Role of the Grandparent

Following the death, your role in the family will probably be to make yourself available to others. You may need to be present for moral support—to soothe, to perform practical assistance, and to listen endlessly as the same stories are repeated again and again. You have probably shared in your grandchild's life from the very beginning, so you will be a good person to listen to stories. You may remember the way little Johnny couldn't pronounce his "S's" or his refusal to call his baby sister by her name until she was three years old. Or you may simply be needed as a sounding board, patiently listening to family history. Happy memories will be important during this time. You can use them to help fill the void left by your loss.

I wanted to go to sleep and wake up to find it had all been a bad dream. The possibility of living the

rest of my days without my grandchild was too
awful to even think about.

But there is no way to make this nightmare go
away. It is a reality that doesn't disappear.

As a grieving grandparent, remind yourself that
you have suffered the loss of a loved one, too. In
fact, your pain is two-fold—the loss of your grandchild and the pain of watching your own child's
agony. The death of a child or grandchild goes
against the order of nature. Young people are not
supposed to die before their elders. When they do,
it makes everyone extremely aware of their own
mortality. In the face of this unnatural, painful
loss, you will feel powerless and alone.

Feeling powerless or out of control can be frightening. When our well-ordered lives whirl around
like spinning tops, we wish to grab them and
restore them to order. Instead we flounder about
as we come to the realization that we were never
in control in the first place.

This might be an appropriate time to search your
heart and call upon your heavenly Father for direc-
tion. Any child who has lost his way can benefit
greatly from knowing his father is near and guid-
ing him. Likewise, your feeling of abandonment
will lessen as you call upon your heavenly Father
in this time of sorrow.

It is also important to realize that your grieving child will probably not be able to help heal
the hole left in your heart by the loss of your
grandchild. The parents of the child who has died
are usually submerged in their own pain and

have no resources left to draw upon to help others. You may have to seek your solace elsewhere.

The Needs of Your Grief-stricken Child

Grievers often feel fragmented, finding it difficult to perform seemingly simple tasks such as washing a load of laundry or ironing a shirt. You may be needed to keep the household running smoothly unless it is obvious that the grievers wish to be alone. It is often best to take your clues from actions rather than words. Grievers usually do not know their own desires, so they have difficulty expressing them to others. Observe facial expressions and body language before doing anything.

Presence, Assistance, Listening

Place the acronym *PAL* in the back of your mind to help you remember the three most important areas where you can help.

The P stands for Presence.

Your physical presence will be very important. Your warmth and love can wordlessly surround your grieving child. Quietly be there for the family as they face their darkest days.

The A stands for Assistance.

You can assist in practical tasks that may seem overwhelming to your child at this time. The dry cleaning still needs to be picked up, the groceries bought, the children car-pooled. Do whatever you can to lighten the load of daily tasks.

The L stands for Listening.

Listen whenever someone needs to talk. Research shows that the best way to work through grief is by talking about it. Keep this in mind as your child wants to repeat the same stories. I call these the "tapes of grief" that must be played to be believed. Each time grievers play their tapes and hear them, acceptance comes a little closer. Listen to your child's tapes as many times as they need to be played.

Listen also as anger is verbalized, as shattered hopes and dreams are expressed. Don't judge, offer advice, or correct. Simply listen. The gift of unconditional listening is a rare one. When given in love it will be greatly appreciated. Be a *PAL* to your grieving child.

Prayer

Another loving gift you can give to your grieving children is prayer. Prayer is very powerful. Be in constant prayer for your loved ones. They will be able to feel the strength and comfort of the Lord when nothing else can penetrate their pain. Pray for answers and guidance in all that you do even if your own faith may be faltering at this time due to the pain of your own loss.

Fay Angus writes, "'Faith is the bird that sings to greet the dawn while it is still dark.'

"If we take that Indian proverb, and through the dark night of our soul learn to sing its song of faith, we break the pain of heartache and stir the promise of the morning light."[1] Prayer can be our song in the darkest night as we wait for dawn to appear.

It is in our most desperate hours that God will reach out his arms in consolation.

"He is like a father to us, tender and sympathetic to those who reverence him" (Ps. 103:13). If ever you needed that tenderness and sympathy, it's now!

Patience

As you watch your grieving child, you might be tempted to rush the healing process because of your own pain. It is difficult for parents to stand by and watch their children in agony. You may unconsciously desire to rush them through the steps of healing for your own comfort because watching them suffer is just too hard.

I know my mom couldn't bear to see me in so much pain, so she was always making suggestions for ways to make myself feel better. I know she meant well, but to tell me to get my hair done or buy a new dress and I'd feel better only irritated me and made me feel like she didn't understand at all. It wasn't until years later that I could understand that these suggestions were coming from her own heartache. She wanted me to be fine again so she could feel better. It was a vicious circle.

Try not to allow this kind of "vicious circle" to begin. Back off if you see signs of it and ask your child genuinely, *What would you like me to do?* Then follow those particular suggestions. Needs can change without warning, and the assistance that seemed to help one week may be outdated the next.

While this is going on, you will probably feel as if you are on a roller coaster. Only this ride never seems to end. That's exactly what your grieving child is feeling, too. When on a roller coaster, if someone sits next to you and holds your hand it is not as scary. You can take on the role of the one who holds the hand whenever it seems as if there is nothing else that can be done.

Practical Helps

Grieving parents may appreciate notes from their parents more than phone calls. The telephone can become an enemy to a household with a recent loss. It seems to ring constantly, interrupting conversations, thought processes, or just badly needed quiet time. Talking to others is often exhausting and draining; therefore, notes that arrive in the mail serve the purpose of letting grievers know that they are loved and being prayed for, but do not require a response like a telephone call does.

One young woman said that after her mother left town to return to her own home, she found notes her mother had tucked in various places for many weeks. Each time she found one in the bottom of a drawer or inside her Bible, she felt nurtured and loved.

Flowers or inexpensive gifts can convey your love also. Or, if you live nearby, an offer of making dinner once a week until life settles back into a routine is greatly appreciated. However, practical assistance needs to be offered with no expectations in return. One grandmother said she had the key to her daughter's house and several times a week she left dinner in the oven ready to be reheated. In that way, she was providing a service, but not draining energy from her daughter's family or interfering with their own schedule in any way.

It may be helpful to read some books on grief and make them available to the other grievers in the family. Check the reference section at the back of this book for suggestions.

When a Baby Dies

Miscarriage and Stillbirth

There is nothing so precious as a newborn baby. Parents and grandparents alike wait anxiously for the arrival of a new family member. If that pregnancy results in a miscarriage or a stillbirth, grandparents hurt right along with the prospective parents. However, there isn't usually much of an opportunity to grieve the loss of such a little one. Life goes on in a normal manner; the sun still shines, defying the dark clouds in your hearts. As a grandparent, you will probably not receive flowers, sympathy cards, or caring words, unless you have been blessed with some very special friends.

It is important that your child knows how much you care and that you felt this baby was a very special one whether it was full term or not. Express that you understand that this little person will never be replaced with another one exactly like him. If the baby was given a name, use it when talking to your child. Make yourself available to balance the scales by being considerate and not expecting the parents to bounce back immediately. It will be a process, as with any death, and each person must be given the freedom to complete his or her grief according to his or her own inner clock.

SIDS

When a baby dies from SIDS (sudden infant death syndrome), it is a unique situation. The parents gratefully thought their worries were over with the successful birth of a healthy baby. They are just beginning to enjoy and get to know this new bundle of joy when it is snatched away from them. While they try not to blame themselves, they can't help feeling it was somehow their fault. You need to reassure them while at the same time your own arms are longing to hold that precious little one just one more time.

I have a friend who was holding her seven-week-old grandson when he suddenly stopped breathing. Although well-versed in the procedure for resuscitation, she was unable to revive him. The paramedics were also unable to do anything when they arrived. It was an unusual SIDS death because it did not happen when the baby was asleep in his crib as is usually the case.

Parents of SIDS babies often think if they had checked the baby sooner or had not been sleeping so soundly they could have prevented the death. This particular case shows that even if you are holding a potential SIDS baby there is nothing you can do to prevent the heartbreaking death.

Forgotten Grievers

With most deaths there are going to be forgotten grievers. Forgotten grievers are the people who are not the next of kin, but who are profoundly affected by a death.

Grandparents

Because your relationship is one generation removed from the person who has just died, people may forget you have suffered a great loss. And the older the grandchild, the harder it will be for people to include you among the bereaved.

I spoke with one grandmother whose grandson Tony was in his forties when he died. To the rest of us this was a grown man whose wife and children were grieving terribly. To "Nana" this was the young man who received his first haircut from her. (She still kept his beautiful blonde curl in an envelope in her top drawer.) She had dear memories of him including his prom night when he stopped over to introduce her to his date, the girl he later married.

At the funeral, Nana sat behind Tony's wife and children, two rows over from Tony's elderly parents. Nobody spoke to this frail white-haired woman in the third row, and nobody hugged her or offered condolences.

A grandparent is still a grandparent no matter how old the grandchild is.

If you are grieving a grown grandchild, reach out to others for support. Remind your own friends that you have suffered a loss and share it with your church family. Instead of being hurt by the lack of recognition, ask for help and for hugs. The neglect you are feeling is surely not intentional on the part of your friends. You might also be able to ease your own pain by looking for other forgotten grievers and reaching out to them. Remember, when you give a hug, you also receive one!

Siblings

Forgotten grievers may be found among the other children in the family. Children of all ages are often left by the wayside when a death occurs. The surviving sibling or siblings will need to receive love and support; however, the parents may be too overwhelmed with their own grief to be of much help. An offer from you to do something special with their other children or to have a grandchild spend a few nights at your house might be a great assistance to bereaved parents. Children serve as great distractions when you are overwrought and they can provide a welcome break from constant mourning. Allow the youngsters to express their emotions over the death and to talk about their feelings. Encourage them to ask questions.

When my sister died, my parents were so sad that I felt it would have been better if I had died instead. Then they wouldn't have been as sad.

Children do not seem to realize their own importance and need to be reassured that their parents' grief would be just as intense if they had been the one who had died. They need to be told that their parents' current lack of attention toward them is due to their tremendous pain and should not be misunderstood as an absence of love.

As a grandparent, you can be a great help when this occurs by explaining it to the other grandchildren and giving them some extra nurturing until their parents are able to do so again.

Children need the same things adults need. They need a listening ear, they need to have the details explained so they can more readily understand the reasons behind the death, and they need to be reassured when they are fearful.

Children tend to be egocentric and may think they did something to cause the death. They need enough details to erase these fears. A typical reaction from a child might be: *My brother was riding my bike, therefore it was my fault that the car hit him.* Or, *If I had been nicer to my sister she wouldn't have gotten sick.* Or, *When I pushed my sister down and her knee bled, she got a blood disease that made*

her die. Children who are piecing together over-
heard facts have a greater chance of processing
incorrect information than those who are encour-
aged to talk about their concerns and who have
been told the truth from the beginning.

Children also tend to worry about dying like their
loved one did. They need to have the facts so that
this fear does not grow out of proportion.

When we returned home from his brother's
funeral, I noticed six-year-old Timmy rubbing his
neck. It concerned me because his younger brother
had died from Hodgkin's disease. I crossed the room
to talk to Timmy, stooping down to his eye level.
As we talked I was able to reassure him that many
illnesses are not contagious. I told him that even
though it was easy to catch a cold from someone,
Hodgkin's disease is something one person does
not catch from another. From his expression I knew
I had correctly guessed his concern.

It is necessary for someone to discuss the details
of the events that will take place in the upcoming
days. This task may fall to you. Everything should
be carefully explained in simple language so no
misunderstandings occur. When conversing with
young people, make sure they have a clear de-
finition and not jumbled ideas they have concocted
for themselves. Vague concepts about new words
like mortuary, funeral, and eternity can be con-
fusing. It is a good idea to have young children
repeat the facts you have given them to be sure
they are comprehending and are processing the
information correctly.

When talking with children about death, avoid euphemisms such as "just resting" or "has gone to sleep." Children have been known to ask why Daddy doesn't wake up and go home with them after the funeral, in response to having been told that "Daddy is taking a long nap." Other children have refused to go to bed at night afraid that they, too, will fall asleep and be buried in the ground.

One little boy had been very naughty after the death of his brother. Finally the story came out that he was afraid that if he was good, God would need him for another angel and would take him to heaven like he had his brother. Apparently, someone had told him that God needed another little angel and that was the reason his brother had died.

Dan Schaefer has an excellent book about children and the grief process titled *How Do We Tell the Children?* He writes, "This book will tell you what children aged two and up already know and are capable of understanding about death; what words to use when explaining death, including special situations; and how to help your child deal with grief." This well-written book gives explicit information that can be very valuable in helping children deal with death and even includes a crisis section for quick reference. Schaefer, who was director of a New York funeral home for more than twenty-five years, writes, "I've worked with more than 3,000 parents during the days just after a death, and one thing I know for sure—many people find it almost impossible to talk to their children about death."[2]

In working with grieving teenagers I have found their main concern is usually not to be any different from their peers. The death of a sibling may put them in the spotlight where they least want to be. As their grandparent, you can watch for these uncomfortable situations and be sensitive to the teens' needs, intervening if necessary, on their behalf.

Beth's teenage brother was killed in a motorcycle accident. The first Sunday Beth returned to church all the members of their youth group gathered around her to ask questions. She was still feeling extremely fragile and could not talk about her brother without crying. Her grandmother saw the group across the parking lot and realized Beth was in the center. She quickly assessed the situation and called out to Beth. "Honey, come help me carry these things in, will you?" Beth came running over and gave her a hug and a grateful smile. She had been rescued from the spotlight.

Nurturing Yourself

In addition to ministering to your grieving child and the forgotten grievers, you will need to pay special attention to your own well-being. Remember, you are grieving also, so do not forget to treat yourself gently.

Positive Self-Talk

The way you talk to yourself during this grief process can have a great impact on your recovery.

Begin right now to listen to what you are saying. People believe what they hear; therefore, it is very important to be saying positive, kind, encouraging words to yourself. Tell yourself that you will heal, that each day will be easier, and that joy will return to your life. Give yourself permission to cry when you are feeling sad and to make mistakes. Reassure yourself that you do not need to be perfect and that you are in fact getting better. Begin each day by telling yourself that today will be better and that you are going to be all right.

Good Grooming

In addition to talking to yourself tenderly, try to practice good grooming. After her husband died, Georgia purchased a full-length mirror for her home. Each morning after she dressed, she would look in the mirror and make sure she looked presentable to the outside world, no matter how poorly she felt inside. "The way you look has a great bearing on the way you feel about yourself," she says. "If you know you look as good as you can, you will feel better."

I can attest that Georgia always looks gorgeous! Her silver hair is neatly trimmed, her nails polished, and her outfits color-coordinated. It is a pleasure to see her walk into a room. Georgia claims that you do not have to spend great amounts of money on your clothes; she shops at thrift shops. And, she contends, "A dash of favorite perfume before you leave the house does great things to lift your spirit."

Proper Nutrition

In addition to looking good on the outside, it is essential to eat properly, exercise, get adequate rest, and seek medical care for physical problems. It is easier to cope with your grief if you are in good physical health.

You may not feel like eating or you may find yourself overeating. Both are common ways of dealing with grief. During this time it is especially important to be aware of your eating habits and to try to control them. Good nutrition will contribute to a feeling of well-being. Meals should be eaten on a fairly regular schedule, three times a day, and not simply when you feel like eating. Nibbling away at junk food all day long cannot take the place of well-balanced meals. Some people tell me that stress-formula vitamins also help them feel better.

It is not advisable to turn to alcohol at any time, but especially not when you are grief-stricken and your defenses are already down. A glass of wine at bedtime might sound like a good way to relax before trying to sleep, but alcohol is actually a depressant and can drag you down emotionally. One glass can lead to two, and all the time you will actually be making yourself feel sadder and putting a hindrance in the way of recovery.

Relaxation without Drugs

Grievers, especially, must beware of taking drugs. Drugs, even prescription drugs, will mask true feelings and prevent the natural process of grief. Eventually the drugs must be stopped. At that time, the person is suddenly slammed back to square one of the grief process. The longer the period of time that elapses before this happens, the harder it is to recover. Support systems have most likely vanished with the passage of time so that making a comeback will be an even bigger struggle. It is better to face your grief in a natural way without tranquilizers.

This might be a good time to work on learning relaxation techniques. Search for a book that describes techniques for relaxing your body and improving breathing techniques. Or try this simple exercise: Breathe slowly through your nose, expand your abdomen and then your rib cage. Next, release the breath through your nose more slowly than you took it in, silently counting to eight. Do this several times a day or whenever you find yourself getting especially tense. It really helps!

If you are battling distressing thoughts or pictures that never seem to go away, try a technique called "thought interruption." You may want to devise your own method after experimenting with each of the following:

1. When an upsetting thought keeps churning around in your head, tell yourself, "I am going to sweep this up and get rid of it." Then, mentally picture yourself sweeping it into a dustpan and emptying it into the trash. When the unpleasant thoughts have been tossed out, replace them with prayer or hum an uplifting hymn.

2. Picture a chalkboard. Take an eraser and wipe away the distasteful picture or thought. Now, write a verse of Scripture on the chalkboard or draw a beautiful picture.
3. Take the negative picture or thought and put a television screen around it. Then tell yourself, "Now, I'm going to change the channel." (Or use a remote control if you prefer.) Change the picture to a pleasant one of a sunset or scenic ocean view.

You may have to apply these techniques repeatedly in the beginning until you train yourself to think pleasant thoughts instead of disturbing ones. Talk to yourself whenever distressing thoughts or pictures try to dominate your mind. Use one of the above techniques or the specific one you have developed to change your thought pattern. Then talk to yourself about the alternate pleasant picture you have used for replacement and say, "What a beautiful beach this is that I'm visiting," or, "Look how clean the chalkboard appears before I write down Scripture verses on it." Talk to yourself with encouraging words about pleasant times or places. The important part is not to allow yourself to be consumed with distressing thoughts or pictures. Take control and replace "bad stuff" with helpful images that will aid in your recovery instead of dragging you down.

Exercise

Another way of nurturing yourself is exercise. Daily exercise is one of the best methods for getting your body to feel better and for working off repressed feelings of anger or depression. It also leads to better sleeping and eating patterns. Exercise should not be erratic or excessive. Begin slowly and only with a doctor's permission if you have previous health problems. A short, brisk walk around the block, a few minutes of stretching exercises, or a moderate swim are good ways to begin.

Working in the garden can also provide a good release. There is something about having your hands in dirt and working with plants that is soothing. Feel the sunshine warm your back as you plant seeds or pull out weeds. It will lower your stress level considerably.

Creativity

Turn to creative activities for solace. Whatever your talents or interests may be, put them to use to help heal your grief. Some of the most beautiful music, poetry, and paintings were created during periods of pain for the artist. As Karl Barth noted, "The generation that has no great anguish on its heart will have no great music on its lips."[3] Release your agony by putting it to music or on a canvas.

If possible, encourage the children in the family to express their feelings in the same way. Paint together or sing together. Assist them so their creative processes can get started. Buy them a sketch pad or a notebook to write down their feelings.

Explain to them that nobody has to see their work. It is merely for their own release and pleasure.

Helpful Hints

This is the time for getting plenty of rest and for treating yourself with great kindness. Pamper yourself. Treat yourself to a professional massage, a manicure, or a new hairstyle (or all three!). Buy a new suit or prepare your favorite gooey dessert. Take an entire day and drive to the mountains or to the beach and indulge yourself. It is not selfish to put yourself first when you are grieving; it is a necessity.

Search for good friends or renew old acquaintances that you once enjoyed. Spend time talking, laughing, and reminiscing with special, caring people. There is no better prescription for reviving your spirits. Find friends you feel comfortable crying with—tears shared are twice as soothing as tears shed alone. Allow others to sustain you. Don't be embarrassed to show your weakness as you walk along this difficult path.

2

The Grief Process

*M*any people have tried to explain grief. Following the death of her husband, author Madeleine L'Engle wrote, "It [grief] is like walking through water. Sometimes there are little waves lapping about my feet. Sometimes there is an enormous breaker that knocks me down. Sometimes there is a sudden fierce squall. But I know that many waters cannot quench love, neither can floods drown it."[1]

Grief is the result of loving someone. We do not grieve for anyone we do not love. The only people who can avoid grief are people who never allow themselves to love. The goal of successful grief work is to reach a point where happy, loving memories remain after most of the sadness has been washed away by tears.

Emotional Stages of Grief

When people are grieving, they go through many different stages and experience a wide range of feelings. Emotions closely associated with grief are denial, shock, anger, guilt, fear, and depression. Experts refer to these as "the stages of grief." Not everyone experiences every stage nor do the stages arrive in any special order. They can come all at once in a bundle and stay for a while, or they can be fleeting. People grieve in their own individual ways and on their own time schedules. Allow yourself the freedom to work through the grief process in your own time.

Just as pain in your body must be identified before it can be taken care of, so must painful emotions be identified. Place a name tag on feelings and then ask yourself, *What can I do with this feeling?* When an overwhelming emotion appears on the scene recognize it, decide if it is healthy or destructive, and then if necessary take steps to rectify it. Feelings are neither right nor wrong, so do not chastise yourself if you are experiencing an upsetting emotion such as anger, guilt, depression, or jealousy.

It is important to be able to identify different stages or feelings so that you can feel more in control. You will also be able to recognize these stages in other family members and reassure them that they are normal, that they are not going crazy or losing their minds.

The early days after receiving the news will probably involve some denial followed by shock and numbness.

Denial

When tragic news is received, a certain amount of denial is natural and normal. Our minds refuse to accept the unacceptable. Our first reaction is one of disbelief. "Oh, no, it can't be!" or, "There must be some mistake," are phrases commonly heard following bad news. Our minds do not want to accept the news, so we cushion them by not believing it.

I personally ask numerous questions as I try to move from denial into the next stage. I want all the details as I process the information. Sometimes I have to hear the information several times before I begin to accept it.

After I have gone over the information and processed it clearly, I can move on. For many people, the denial of the truth allows their bodies time to go into shock, which protects them from the initial pain.

Shock and Numbness

Shock is a type of natural, psychological Novocain that nature provides to help grievers get through the beginning of the grief process. With time, this natural anesthetic wears off and reality begins to sink in. This time period will be the most painful. Do not get discouraged if all of a sudden you think you are regressing instead of progressing. This is merely a sign that you are now beginning to function without a natural cushion of protection. Your grown child probably will be experiencing doubts about regression and will need to be reassured that this is a normal result of experiencing your loss without the assistance of the anesthetic of the early days.

This stage often arrives between six weeks and three months following the loss. Suddenly the griever is crying more than ever and interprets these new feelings as a setback when in fact they are a sign of progress. Shock has decreased and genuine feelings are beginning to surface. It is important to understand this phenomenon and not be overcome with feelings of hopelessness. Watch for indications of shock wearing off in your grieving child so you can offer reassurance and hope for the future.

At this time when you and the other grievers think you cannot feel any worse, you will begin to see signs of progress. They will be slight at first, and you will feel like you are taking one step backward for every two steps forward before this whole process is over. However, be reassured that each step forward counts, regardless of how small it might be. I have never seen a person who was grieving *and who wanted to get better* that did not.

Abraham Lincoln said, "In this sad world of ours, sorrow comes to all, and it often comes with bitter agony. Perfect relief is not possible except with time. You cannot now believe that you will ever feel better. But this is not true. You are sure to be happy again. Knowing this, truly believing it, will make you less miserable now."

Anger

Anger is a genuine emotion experienced by grievers. Psychiatrists claim there is no such thing as a person who never gets angry; there are only those people who do not know how to show it. Anger becomes a problem if it is repressed and left to ferment inside. Angry feelings can be frightening because they are often unfamiliar, and unfortunately many of us feel it is unacceptable to show anger. Angry feelings can be compared to taking a deep breath. They cannot be held forever and will not go away until they are released. The longer anger is held inside, the more it will make us feel as if we are going to explode.

Reassure other family members, including any children, that anger is healthy and normal. Try to introduce the subject of anger into conversations so that others will feel comfortable sharing their angry feelings. Try never to contradict an angry person by saying, *You shouldn't be angry about that!* Angry feelings are rarely logical—they simply appear and must be dealt with in an acceptable manner. Taking them out of the closet and airing them verbally is one of the best ways to make them disappear.

Once you recognize anger, figure out *whom* you are angry with or *what* you are angry about. Then, rationally decide where this fury can be channeled. It is important to express your wrath, but to do it in a way that will not be destructive to anyone or anything. The goal is to purge angry feelings at your discretion instead of letting them erupt like a volcano without warning at an inappropriate time or at an undeserving person.

The only grandchild of one of my coworkers, Shirley, died at nine months of age. Everyone was amazed at how well Shirley was handling her devastating loss. I was more concerned than amazed. To me, Shirley looked like a bomb ready to explode. Shirley carried on her duties professionally while all the time her actions seemed more and more tense.

Shirley had a plant on her desk that she had received following the funeral. Each day it wilted a bit more until it was a complete goner. Still it sat on her desk week after week. One morning I glanced up just as Shirley grabbed the plant and heaved it across the room. Then she put her head on her desk and sobbed.

It was the explosion I had been expecting. Shirley needed to release her frustration, anger, and pain. Holding it inside was doing her gross damage, and it finally escaped of its own volition. After a long, hard cry that seemed to come from the depths of her soul, Shirley relaxed and began to look less tense. We reassured her that she could be in control of releasing her anger and did not need to allow it to control her.

Physical exercise is a productive way to vent anger. As you take a vigorous walk around the block, you will begin to feel better. Choose an activity that you previously enjoyed and ask your favorite friend to join you. Or watch for unexpressed anger in loved ones and suggest you work out your feelings together.

Lynn walked around for weeks with her fists clenched and her insides knotted up in anger after her first grandchild died from SIDS. *Why did our little one have to be the one to die? That baby was so well-loved and we waited for him for so long. Why not some unwanted pregnancy to an unmarried teenager instead? We go to church, we love the Lord. Our family didn't deserve this!* On and on her thoughts churned, threatening to tear her to shreds emotionally. One day when she was walking by a lake she stopped and threw a rock into the water. Then she threw another and another until she was hurling them with all her might. "Take that, and that and that," she screamed at the water.

She threw the rocks until she was exhausted and yelled until she was hoarse. Then she headed home. It was the best afternoon she had experienced since little Jamie's death. As tired as she was, she felt cleansed and at peace.

Another good way to rid yourself of rage is through writing. Write down the reasons for your anger, getting them down on paper and out of your head, and away from your system. Use any creative means you choose—music, artwork, or dance—but continue to work at it for as long as it takes for you to feel at peace again.

It does not make any difference what kind of cleansing activity you choose for tossing away the furor you have stored up inside, but it is important to throw it away instead of hanging on to it.

When you have found a successful means of expressing your own anger, share this with your loved ones in the hopes that it may also work for them. The important part is to not repress angry feelings.

Guilt

Guilt is another emotion that hovers about grievers, disturbing their peace of mind and well-being. You may feel guilty about any number of things that are real or imagined. Guilty feelings stand in the way of healing. Guilt pulls people down into an ocean of despair and prevents them from surfacing until they drown. Guilt, like anger, does not go away simply because it is ignored. It only grows more disruptive, depleting your energy and healthy growth.

If you are able to talk to someone about your guilt, hearing it expressed can often make it seem less valid. Try to talk to someone who is not judgmental and who will be a good listener as you sort out your feelings for yourself. Support groups are excellent for this.

Thoughts or verbal sentences that begin with the words *If only, I should have,* and *Why didn't I* can only be destructive. The past cannot be changed. Nevertheless we can learn from it in the hopes of preventing the same mistakes again. In the future we need to listen to the way we talk to ourselves and then make an effort to be more tender and to treat ourselves more kindly. When we forgive ourselves we can begin to move forward instead of backward.

It may be important to help your grieving child expel guilty feelings also. Do not tell him he has no reason to feel guilty. Guilt feels very real and needs to be expressed. Encourage conversation about any unexpressed guilt and listen with a non-critical ear. Show that you understand the feelings without acknowledging that they are either correct or incorrect. As you listen while your loved one expresses feelings, he or she may be able to reconcile his or her own guilt.

Write your personal guilty feelings on paper and then tear up the paper to visibly rid yourself of them. Suggest other family members do likewise. Remember that guilty feelings do not become part of you unless you are willing to accept them. As they creep into the recesses of your mind, send them away. Replace them with pleasant thoughts and prayer, forcing them to move farther away from you.

Fear

C. S. Lewis said, "No one ever told me grief felt so like fear. I am not afraid, but the sensation is like being afraid."[2] Fear can play a very active part in the grief process. Often, as C. S. Lewis stated, anxiety will *feel* like fear, but you are not actually fearful of anything specific.

If you are feeling afraid, take the time to think your feelings through. Ask yourself some questions:

Am I exaggerating the situation?
Have I expressed my fear verbally?
Have I confronted my fear to see if it is legitimate?
If the fear is legitimate, have I taken steps to rectify it or am I just worrying about it?
Have I prayed about the situation and handed it over to the Lord?

Try writing down your fears. Then tear up the paper, and throw it out, symbolizing that your fears are thrown away just as you did with your guilty feelings. Or admit to a trusted friend or relative that you are feeling afraid. Often, simply getting fear out in the open will make it disappear or diminish. Fears that are shared decrease in importance.

Depression

Depression may surround you like a tight kid glove. You want to remove it, but may not have the strength to pull it off. Depression is probably the most common symptom of grief and is one that attacks every griever in one form or another. It may be the result of unresolved anger or a combination of physical symptoms and other grief-related emotions, such as guilt, that are very draining. Often grievers are having problems with good nutrition or insomnia. They are not eating or sleeping properly so they feel drained and listless. This lack of energy contributes to depression.

If guilt is eating away at a person, it will also sap his or her energy and allow depression to move in. Depression is a smothering emotion that often prevents people from making any progress in their grief work.

Research has shown that our physical bodies are at their lowest ebb between two and three o'clock in the morning. People who are grieving are in a perpetual state of "three o'clock in the morning." Grievers have no leftover resources available to cope with everyday problems. Depression sneaks in and pulls them down lower and lower.

In order to cure depression you must take action; therefore, it is important to recognize signs of depression before they become debilitating. This looks easy on paper, but one of the signs of depression is a low energy level, so beginning any activity can be extremely difficult. It is best to think small and start gradually. As you start to benefit from the activity it should become easier to increase your time and exertion.

Physical exercise can generate the body's natural healing process. When you are grieving you are in the process of healing a broken heart. Take advantage of the opportunity to help mend your body by doing some gentle, mild exercises. You might begin with a short walk or a few simple stretching exercises. Small goals are preferable in the beginning because they allow for success and do not stress an already overloaded system. Check with a physician before attempting anything you have never done previously or if you have health conditions that prohibit exercise.

With normal grief there is a feeling of melancholy, a lack of energy, and little interest in life. However, keep in mind that depression cannot thrive when it is verbally expressed. Find a trusted friend, relative, support group, or therapist and express your feelings. Admitting you are heartsick, simply saying it out loud, can be a first step on the path to easing depression.

If you have never kept a daily journal, this is a good time to start. (Use pages 86–96 to begin.) Write out your feelings each day and then every once in a while look back over the entries. Ruth tells me that four years later, she can distinguish her black times from her gray ones until at last she reached pure white ones. As she looks at her progress it lifts her spirits to see how far she has come. Try it!

Listen to your internal dialogue for *Why me?* questions. In the early days of grief, it is necessary to think through your loss thoroughly. Thinking about it will help you to accept it. However, after a while you will need to move beyond the questions. Take the useless *Why me?* questions and turn them into a more helpful *How.*

Change *Why did this have to happen to me?* to *How can I put this experience to good use?* Or, *How can I help someone else with a similar loss?* Instead of, *Why am I so miserable?* ask, *How can I resolve my feelings of sadness and begin to move forward?* Hear the difference? *Why* is negative and *how* is positive. It is important to pull positive responses forward so you can begin to mend.

A support group can be very helpful while you are going through these feelings because it will reassure you that your feelings are normal and that you are not alone in your suffering. Others are experiencing the same feelings and will nod their heads across the table, letting you know they feel the same way.

Depression will surely visit your house, but that does not mean you have to make it a welcome guest. Don't allow depression to be in charge of your life. Send it away with mild exercise, uplifting music, or some other creative outlet.

A word of caution: Spending days in bed without eating or making any effort at personal care, uncontrolled crying that continues for weeks or for the majority of the day even weeks after the death, thinking of ways to end life and stockpiling pills, or reading up on methods of suicide are signs of extreme depression. If any of these things occur the person needs immediate professional help. These feelings are beyond normal depression.

Physical Symptoms of Grief

Listlessness

Following the death of a loved one you will probably feel tired most of the time. You may have little or no energy and find it difficult to be enthusiastic about any task or project. You might listlessly do what is required of you, but experience no joy from completing any jobs. Social events that you once relished may now seem dull. Church attendance often means soaking three tissues per service. You wake up tired in the morning and drag about all day waiting to sleep again only to repeat the process.

Inability to Concentrate

Your attention span is often exceedingly short. You read two pages of a book and lose interest. You may read parts of the newspaper and not remember a word you have read. You write yourself notes and then forget where you put them. You get lost on a route you have driven daily, forget where you are headed, burn your dinner, and injure yourself frequently. You will feel frustrated, clumsy, and stupid. These are all natural parts of the grief process.

Lack of Willpower

It will probably take all your willpower to cook dinner each night, and the food will have little or no appeal to you. Good nutrition is especially important for grievers. You need every source possible to regain your strength. Try to eat well-balanced meals and avoid overindulging.

Poor Sleep Habits

Sleep habits may become erratic or disturbed. Unless absolutely necessary, do not resort to sleeping pills. Sleeping pills can be addictive and do not provide the same quality of sleep that natural sleep does. If you are having difficulty sleeping, try natural aids instead of drugs for inducing sleep. Drinking a glass of warm milk, listening to soothing music, reading quietly, or praying are all good ways to relax as you prepare for sleep. Avoid getting overstimulated close to bedtime and choose your activities carefully.

Susceptibility to Illness

You may notice you have an unusually low resistance to illness. Germs seem to seek you out. It feels as if it takes forever to recover from a cold, and then you quickly catch another one. Toothaches appear, or backaches, or shortness of breath. You feel you have aged twenty years in two weeks' time. All these symptoms are a normal part of the grief process too.

It is a good idea to seek medical care to verify that you do not have a serious illness in addition to your grief. Explain the situation to your physician so that he or she can help you to feel the best that you possibly can. Often simply being reassured that you have nothing seriously wrong with you will take away the worry and allow you to feel a bit better.

Observe other family members, especially the children, and make sure they are taken care of physically during this time. They have fewer inner resources to draw upon and will need you to reassure them that they are not dying or experiencing anything abnormal. Abundant hugs and touching can ease much of the physical trauma of grief. Don't be afraid to ask for and give hugs!

Crying

You may cry over nothing and over everything. Crying is good for you. Tears can speak when there are no words to express the way you are feeling and can offer a release of all your pent-up pain. Compassion and understanding are bred from tears.

"Crying is one of the healthiest things you can do," writes Bob Deits. "Studies have shown that tears of sadness have a different chemical makeup than tears of joy. Tears of sadness release substances that have a calming effect. It is no myth that you feel better after a good cry. Tears are also one of the signs that you are beginning the process of recovery."[3]

Tears can release tension. They can literally wash away sadness. After a good, hard cry, force yourself to do something constructive such as exercising, writing, singing, or scrubbing the kitchen floor. The combined release will lower your stress level considerably.

My friend Barbara recently told me that when she asked her mother how she was doing following the death of a loved one, her mother told her she was crying buckets of tears. I was touched when Barbara said she responded by asking her mother, "Won't you let me help you carry those buckets?" What a generous offer! I'm going to try to always be available to help carry my grieving friends' buckets of tears.

Matthew 5:4 says, "Blessed are those who mourn, for they shall be comforted" (RSV). Allowing tears to flow gives others an opportunity to offer comfort to your wounded spirit. God is there with you in the "valley of the shadow of death" and will comfort you also. God understands crying. "You have seen me tossing and turning through the night. You have collected all my tears and preserved them in your bottle! You have recorded every one in your book" (Ps. 56:8). Every one of your tears is seen and recorded by God. He is there to comfort you whenever you ask.

The Timetable of Grief

The most frequently asked question in regard to the grief process is "When will I stop hurting?" When life is topsy-turvy and you feel out of control, you are naturally anxious to return to normal. If someone could give you a printed time schedule, it would make life much easier. You would know exactly when you could resume normal activities.

The problem is that there is no *normal* where grief is concerned, and there is no set time schedule. Grief takes as long as it takes for each person and each situation. It cannot be rushed and it cannot be put on a back shelf while you simply wait for time to pass. The mere passage of time will not ease the pain; it is the work that is going on during the passing of time that is doing the actual healing. There is no shortcut around it; you must walk right through the center of it, allowing natural healing to occur.

Look to others outside your family for strength and encouragement rather than to family members. It is often difficult for two grievers to be able to help each other. Each has a crippled spirit that needs a sturdy crutch to lean on as the healing takes place. Take the strength that you receive from outside sources and use it as a soothing ointment to your wounded soul. Take advantage of any quiet lulls and use them to reach out and comfort whoever else in your family is in need of solace at each particular moment.

You might suggest quiet walks on the beach where no conversation is necessary as the sound of the waves and the warmth of sunshine on your back renews your spirit. Look for peaceful locations such as monasteries, botanical gardens, or other places where the beauty of nature is abundant. Invite your grieving loved ones to go with you for short outings. Get out the maps and tour books for your area and be creative in planning a special day.

You will experience inner peace as you participate in a refreshing family activity together. Grievers get tired of conversation and appreciate silent moments of respite that are offered by caring friends or relatives.

Your Child's Grief

Your child will probably be experiencing all the symptoms you are experiencing but to a greater degree. There will be the constant reminders, such as setting one less place at the table for dinner, that will not be affecting your life, but will be affecting your child's.

Supporting through Love

It is important to be sensitive to the changes that are taking place and not to expect great leaps of progress from day to day. Mary, whose five-year-old was killed by a hit-and-run driver, said it took her seven years to surface and feel like a "normal human being." During those seven years, she had another child, divorced, remarried, and changed careers.

I acted like a functioning person. But my head was all crazy. I was going through the motions, but not really aware of anything I was doing. It was like a dream where I was watching myself—not real life.

Mary said advice from anyone during this time period fell on deaf ears. She needed to heal in her own way, and the most important support during this time came in the form of love. She wasn't seeking approval or advice, but she certainly needed love. She remembers the hugs and the caring notes she received. They were the only things that kept her going.

I tuned out lectures from my parents and I deserted friends who claimed they knew what was best for me. I searched for people who simply accepted me with all my failings and made me feel I was lovable anyway. I also liked to be with people who didn't know about my son so that when I was with · them I could pretend the accident had never happened. That was the biggest attraction to my second husband. He had never met or known Scotty.

If your child begins to act strangely or does things that are out of character, it will be extremely difficult for you to refrain from offering assistance. However, your advice will probably be ignored, and you will end up estranged when you most want to be available for support. Try to avoid judging behavior unless it is life-threatening (suicide threats or drug addiction, for instance) and merely wait on the sidelines with open arms ready to welcome the lost sheep back into the fold. According to Larry Yeagley,

> The fabric of family unity weakens and crumbles when all family members are expected to grieve in the same way or at the same pace. A grieving person should never feel cut off from his or her family. Some general understanding within the family will facilitate adjustment and prevent this cutting off process.
>
> With continuing honesty, openness and patience, the chances of a family growing together through a loss are great. A family will never be the same after a loss, but hopefully, the positive aspects of recovery will far outweigh the negative side effects.[4]

Avoiding Clichés

As you have probably already experienced, speaking in clichés or platitudes seems to be the biggest "don't" as far as grievers are concerned. They hear so many of them in the days following their loss that they grit their teeth or cringe every time someone tells them, *Time heals all wounds, It's in God's hands,* or *Let me know if there's anything I can do to help.*

Avoid clichés. Grievers would prefer to hear a simple, sincere, *I'm sorry* or *I'm praying for you* rather than an empty, overworn platitude.

With the death of a child, there are many incorrect, hurtful things that people say such as, *God needed another little angel,* or *Be glad you have other children,* or if the loss is a baby, *You can always have more children.* Every child is special and should be treated as a precious individual. These statements deeply pierce an already wounded heart.

If you overhear your child being told such hurtful things, you can run interference or counteract these phrases later with more comforting ones. Reassure your child that nobody would intentionally hurt them. It is simply that many people are uncomfortable with death and don't know how to act or what to say, so they fall back on clichés.

Likewise grandparents may be subjected to thoughtless dialogue from people who do not know what to say. You will have to dig deep into the well of forgiveness and try to forget the extra bruises your heart is being forced to endure.

When this happens, whisper encouraging words to yourself and lean heavily on the Lord for comfort.

The Future

*Y*ou may wonder what the future holds. At times it may seem as if you will never again be as carefree as you once were. It is true that life changes with the death of a loved one; however, that does not mean that life will never again be good. Gradually the day will come when you will notice that sprinkles of joy have crept in to break up your solid mass of sadness.

Growth through Change

Changes will have taken place in the family structure that may have brought everyone closer together and brought about changes in priorities. Your family will now be more compassionate and sensitive.

Judy Tattlebaum writes, "As we journey through these painful experiences of living, we must never forget that we have an amazing resilience and capacity to survive. Just as whole forests burn to the ground and eventually grow anew, just as spring follows winter, so it is nature's way that through it all, whatever we suffer, we can keep on growing. It takes courage to believe we can survive, that we will grow. It takes courage, too, to live now and not postpone living until some vague tomorrow."[1]

The depth of your suffering stems from the same sensitivity that allows a great depth of joy after healing is completed. Never to feel pain means you are so callous that you are also unable to experience happiness.

The crying you have done has melted the frozen walls around your inner being and now little rays of sunshine can filter in, warming your soul. You will almost feel guilty for feeling so good. Days will pass and the death of your grandchild will no longer occupy every waking thought. Your sadness will be fleeting rather than all-encompassing.

This is the time to tell yourself that it is all right to feel good; this is what your grandchild would have wanted. It is time for happy memories to replace gloom. It might also be a good time to go through photographs and make a collage of pleasant days and smiling faces.

Allow your joy to give you strength, but do not be surprised if your child is not at the same spot of recovery that you are. Be careful not to preach or to compare, and by all means do not allow your joy to be so obvious that it acts as salt in your grieving child's wounds.

Grief Spasms

I'll be going along just fine, thinking maybe better days are ahead, when all of a sudden something will trigger a memory and I will burst into tears.

Along with tranquil times come unexpected moments of sudden tears or deep pain. These unexpected times can be thought of as "grief spasms." They arrive exactly as a muscle spasm would—without warning and with great intensity. With a muscle spasm, you would certainly not force yourself into immediate action. Instead you would proceed carefully, coddling the tender spot until it healed. Just as with a muscle spasm, a grief spasm needs to be treated gently until it has passed; pampering is definitely required. Give in to the grief spasms and reassure yourself that they are normal and natural.

Forgiveness

Lack of forgiveness can stand in the way of complete healing. Search your heart and recognize any areas where forgiveness may be necessary. Holding firmly to unforgiveness results in bitterness that will continue to force your already raw wounds to open further.

Blaming God

It may be God you are holding a grudge against. Being angry with God can be a lonely and frightening experience. If you are experiencing this, have an honest talk with God. Tell him the way you feel and your reasons. Ask to be shown a way to be restored to a good relationship. Sit quietly in God's presence or seek out prayer partners who can assist you each day until you are reconciled. I believe God understands these periods of estrangement and wants to help us through them. Do not remain separated from such an important source of consolation at a time when you need it so badly.

Forgiving Others

Do you blame another person for the death of your loved one? If you are blaming a specific person for the death of your grandchild, pray about it. I have seen situations where it seemed as if forgiveness would be impossible, but with time and the grace of God, forgiveness did occur. Ask your trusted Christian friends to pray about it as well. It might help to sit with paper and pencil and make a list of persons you feel you need to forgive.

Dan, whose wife was brutally murdered by her ex-husband, was a member of one of my bereavement groups. Dan had to forgive himself first for not being able to prevent the murder. Then he had to forgive the murderer before he could begin to heal. I knew it was an impossible thing to request of any human being, so I prayed for Dan to receive a forgiving heart. I knew that only with divine intervention would it be possible for Dan to forgive such a horrendous crime.

I asked many people to pray along these lines for Dan, and we left it in God's hands. Within a few weeks' time Dan noticed a softening of his heart, which surprised him as much as it did the rest of us. We had known all along that God was hearing our prayers and that they would be answered; however, we did not expect the results to come so quickly!

One Sunday in church, Dan stood up in front of the congregation and told them that he forgave his wife's murderer and that he was even praying for the man's salvation. Dan's facial expression reflected love, and left no doubt to his sincerity.

Forgiving Yourself

Forgiving yourself is just as important as forgiving someone else. Are you feeling guilty about something you did or said? Are you feeling responsible in any way for the death of your grandchild? Are you carrying around a heavy load that is unnecessary? Pray that you will be able to forgive yourself and ask the Lord to show you any areas that may be standing in the way of your complete healing. Gently remind yourself that the past cannot be changed and that you must move forward instead of backward.

It is important to work on the area of forgiveness because the bitterness of unforgiveness produces a parasite that feeds off a griever and steals peace, comfort, and energy. This results in delayed healing. We want to weed out anything that may prevent healthy growth.

Filling the Void

Wherever there is a loss, there will be loneliness. You will miss the physical presence of your loved one. Sometimes it will be a little dull ache, and other times it will be an engulfing void.

Talk about Your Loss

It is impossible to have your grandchild back physically in your life, but there are a few little tricks for easing loneliness. First, face these early periods of loneliness bravely and do not ignore them. Talk to yourself about the feelings you are experiencing and allow yourself to think about your grandchild. Then, try to remember happy times and cherish those memories as a way to ease your emptiness. Have a memory hour set aside at a specific time each day or each week when you will look at photos, take out remembrances, and think about your grandchild.

Find a trusted person who will understand and be willing to listen as you talk about your loss and about the vacuum you are currently feeling in your life.

Attend a Support Group

Most communities offer grief or bereavement support groups. Check your local newspaper or call hospice, area hospitals, or the Chamber of Commerce about details. I believe support groups are the best way for a griever to be nurtured and assisted in the process of healing. To be able to share your innermost feelings with others who understand your pain brings some relief by knowing your experiences are normal. I have led grief support groups for hospice organizations and for my church for the last ten years.

Grievers have a tendency to feel isolated and alone in their grief. Therefore, it is reassuring to know their suffering is shared by others. To look into tearful eyes across a table and hear someone say, "I understand," and know they really do, lessens the loneliness.

One time Sharon, the mother of a sixteen-year-old girl who was killed by a drunk driver, sat and listened to a nearly hysterical teenager tell about her miscarriage. I couldn't help but think the depth of their grief was entirely different. I confess to thinking the teenager knew nothing about grief and it should have been Sharon who was devastated. Yet Sharon sat listening intently, seeming at peace.

When the teenager finished talking, Sharon took a deep breath and spoke. She expressed a mother's pain and told the young woman how sorry she was that she had been cheated out of ever knowing her child. "It's never easy to lose a child," she said. "My heart goes out to you." Sharon was going to recover and use her pain to help others, easing her own grief each time she did so.

Look for a support group where you too can share with others who understand. Give yourself the opportunity to work out your grief.

Be Creative

If you are at all creative, this might be a good time to take art lessons, cake decorating, or music lessons. Look into classes at your local college or at the arts and crafts supply stores. You will meet others with a common interest and possibly strike up new friendships, in addition to learning a new craft and enriching your life.

You might put together a creative piece of memory in the form of a collage, a piece of music, a poem, or some other form of handiwork or artwork. In the pioneer days women made "grief quilts." As they sat and stitched with friends, they worked out their grief. One woman made a quilt of scraps of material that had been used in articles of clothing for her daughter.

I have held a cross-stitched picture of a shepherd with the inscription, *Suffer the little children to come unto me,* crafted by a mother grieving the death of her young son. Another project done in the throes of grief was a large latch-hook rug that various family members worked on when they needed quiet time alone. I have seen tear-stained pages of poetry and watched a man hammer out his grief while he replaced his shingle roof.

Reach Out

I have seen two lonely people reach across the table at a grief support group and join hands in friendship. I know an elderly woman who is raising a guide dog for the blind, and another who is helping a sick neighbor. All these are ways people have discovered to ease their loneliness.

As time passes and you have worked through some of the pain of the early stages of grief, seek ways to work out your solitary existence by helping others. Following the death of his wife, my uncle would go to the cemetery when he was feeling desolate. "I don't go there to be with Bea," he told me, "I go there to look for others who are sad and lonely and I try to be there for them to talk to or cry with. You can find some real sad people who need comforting in cemeteries, and I always feel better when I return home."

The world is filled with sad, forlorn people who would love to have a friend. Instead of waiting for someone to reach out to you, you can make the first move. Search the newspaper for requests for volunteers, check with your church secretary for shut-ins who need visitors, look into visiting at convalescent homes, hospice, or hospitals. There are two ways to live your life: in the past with regret, or in the future working toward a goal. The choice is up to you.

Write a Letter

Another way to fill the void left in your life is to write letters. This is also a good way to put closure to a relationship where there was no chance to say good-bye. You might use the opportunity to write letters simply as a way of nurturing yourself. The letter can be to yourself clarifying your feelings, it can be a letter to God asking for help, or it can be a letter to your loved one who has died.

I thought I would feel silly writing a letter to my grandbaby who had died at only two weeks of age. Instead, I found myself pouring out all my hopes and dreams that never had a chance to be fulfilled. I was able to express all the love I was feeling on those tear-stained pages. I felt so good after the first letter that I began to write one whenever my empty arms ached.

Another grandmother wrote a love letter to her two-year-old grandson, placed it in a helium balloon, and released it on his birthday. The writing, followed by the release, brought about double therapy for her intense grief.

If you are experiencing a period where you feel as if you are spinning your wheels and not getting anywhere, putting your feelings on paper in the form of a letter may be the added impetus to get you moving forward again.

The letter does not need to be mailed. It is not the reading of the letter that is therapeutic, but the writing of it. Knowing nobody will ever read it gives you the freedom to be perfectly honest and deal with deep feelings you may not have realized existed.

Build a Support System

Judy Tattlebaum in *The Courage to Grieve* writes about the importance of a strong support system. She believes that few of us have an adequate support system for times of crisis: "How we help ourselves through grief very much depends on our self-support, our environmental support and our belief system. In order to be a creative survivor, it is essential that we fully develop all the supports available to us, both to enhance the quality of our lives and as insurance for future times when we may be in great need."[2]

It is good insurance to have a strong support system ready *before* it is needed. We should begin to build a strong support system for ourselves when the memory of our trial is still fresh in our minds. We can evaluate the strengths and weaknesses of our personal support system and then reinforce or build onto any weak area so that the next time we are dealt a major calamity, we will be prepared to face it.

For example, Betty and her husband Bob had no children, so they babied each other to an extreme. After they both retired from their jobs they did everything as a joint effort. They cooked, cleaned house, and ran errands together. When they finished their work, they would play. They golfed, bowled, and worked on their home-built airplane. It was a happy, ideal situation until Betty suddenly died one day. Bob had no friends or family to console him. He had no job to go to each day and he had no church support. Every place he went, and every little chore he did around the house, reminded him of Betty. He fell into a deep state of depression before finding our grief support group.

Fortunately, the other members understood his pain and loneliness and became his lifeline. Bob was an extreme example of allowing all his support to be in a single place, with Betty, and when she was unavailable he had nowhere else to turn.

It is never too soon to look at our support system and to begin to expand it. We can begin to nurture friendships, join a church, or participate in an activity where we can help others who will then be ready to help us when needed. We can make an effort to become acquainted with our neighbors and assist them whenever we can so that we are building a support system for the days ahead.

Have you ever noticed that trees send many roots deep into the ground that hold them steady and firm when storms hit? Their intricate root systems also provide them with nourishment as they thrive and grow. If a tree had only one root, it could easily become diseased or damaged, destroying the entire tree. Like trees, we too need to develop deep, sturdy roots to secure us during the times when storms attack.

Laugh

Laughter is also an important part of the grief process. It can be a balm that soothes an aching soul. People who are grieving often feel guilty if they laugh or enjoy themselves. Nobody can be sad all the time. It is healthy to take a break from grief and release some tension. Give yourself permission to watch a humorous movie or read a comical book. Spend time with friends who are optimistic and lighthearted and absorb some of their joy.

The grief support group I facilitate often shares funny stories so we can take a break from sadness and lighten up a little bit. I do not believe there is a nicer sound to my ears than the first time a grief support group laughs together.

The best jokes are often on ourselves, so I ask for "true confessions" of events that have taken place in their grief process. I sometimes share stories I have heard over the years, such as the one about a woman who drove through a car wash with all her windows down and had to return home to her family drenched from head to toe and "fess up" to her mistake.

Another woman told us she had locked her keys in the car three days in a row. But she proudly announced that she hadn't done that on the fourth day. No, that day she locked them in the trunk!

When I share these stories, I usually need to reassure the group that there is nothing wrong with laughing. It is actually healthy, because it releases the body's natural painkillers (endorphins) and serves to release stress and tension.

Your Child's Continued Needs

While you are healing, what is going on with your child? Your child may be taking small steps toward recovery similar to the ones you are taking or he or she may be moving along at a different pace entirely. Remember that no two people grieve in exactly the same way or on the same schedule.

When your grieving child is having a bad day, he or she does not need the added burden of your worrying over his or her condition. Reassure him that both the good and bad days are natural and normal and that you can handle either one that he may be presently experiencing. A grieving person should not have to dredge up the energy to place a happy mask on her face to protect a loved one from her pain.

In addition to reassurances, you will have to tread quietly and gently around your child's feelings. Continue to provide a listening ear when needed and allow your child the freedom to grieve in his or her particular way. Keep your shoulders available for leaning on or for crying on.

Danger Signs

Although I have stressed the freedom of each person to grieve in his or her own way, there are limits that can be crossed that indicate life is out of control and intervention is needed.

Watch for extremes in your own behavior and in that of your grieving loved ones. For instance, when a person *occasionally* expresses the desire not to go on living, it is a normal reaction to grief. When life seems too painful to endure people will sometimes express a desire to join their loved one in death. If a person wakes up occasionally wishing he did not have to go on, that is normal. However, if someone is trying to devise ways to end his or her life, this is certainly an extreme reaction and a definite danger sign. Any thoughts or mention of suicide should be taken seriously. Professional intervention is necessary under these circumstances.

If such a situation occurs, it is wise to remove weapons, medications, or anything else that may be dangerous in the hands of a suicidal person. Check with a professional if any prescription drugs are currently being taken and find out if they could be contributing to depression and suicidal tendencies.

Alcohol abuse has a way of finding people with a weakness for it during their darkest hours. If alcohol use is excessive and you feel it is causing harm, talk to a trusted friend and seek help.

Watch for extreme changes of sleeping or eating patterns or an extreme drop in performance. Normal grieving is a rough process with many ups and downs; however, do not be fooled into thinking that any deviant behavior is normal. A griever is very fragile and vulnerable and sometimes has to be protected from himself.

Observe the children in the family and make sure they are progressing normally as well. Children usually adjust well to both the process of dying and death if they are included and if the channels are kept open so they feel comfortable expressing their fears and asking questions. Watch for these simple signs that could indicate that trouble is brewing:

1. Notice any sudden personality changes.
2. Observe eating and sleeping habits (for drastic pattern changes).

3. Watch for changes in schoolwork or behavior.
4. Listen for obsessive concern over their own health.
5. Crying easily or being unusually stoic can indicate problems.[3]

Holidays and Other Special Days

Unfortunately, during the period of grief, life continues. Holidays arrive right on schedule, and calendar pages still have to be turned. Just when you are beginning to cope with your loss, along comes an anniversary, a birthday, Thanksgiving Day, or another holiday. Trying to ignore the fact that these dates are approaching does not make them go away.

It is best to meet any holiday head-on dressed in the proper armor so that you will not be caught off guard. Turning your back and pretending it will go away will only make you more vulnerable. Admit up front that holidays will be different now. They may be tearful times for some family members, or they may be somber affairs with bruised hearts meeting other bruised hearts.

Talk about holidays with other family members and make specific plans well in advance. Talk about keeping the traditions the same versus changing them a little bit or completely. Find out what will make each person the least uncomfortable. This is no time for surprises when you and your loved ones are so fragile. Proper preparation and good communication will help you get through these times with the least amount of stress.

Be forewarned that some holidays involve more than just a single day. For instance, Thanksgiving Day plans will be necessary, but do not forget that Friday may also be a holiday for some family members. If you are not working that day, it will be necessary to have definite plans to carry you through a three-day weekend.

The week between Christmas and New Year's can be the same situation. Often people get through the actual holiday, but then have a letdown following it if the remaining time is not structured in some way. Don't put yourself in a position where you will be exposed to more pain than is necessary.

The anniversary of the death, the birthday of your grandchild, any special family day will be especially difficult for the first few years. Be sure your family members are tuned in to each other and everybody has a plan of action for making it through that particular day.

Most people find it better to be in the company of loved ones and spend their time doing something meaningful together in memory of their missing loved one. A trip to the cemetery, a time of quiet fellowship, or sharing memories can reinforce the strength that is gained from loved ones joining together.

Ecclesiastes 4:9–12 tells about the strength of a triple-braided cord. "Two can accomplish more than twice as much as one, for the results can be much better. If one falls, the other pulls him up; but if a man falls when he is alone, he's in trouble.

Also, on a cold night, two under the same blanket gain warmth from each other, but how can one be warm alone? And one standing alone can be attacked and defeated, but two can stand back-to-back and conquer; three is even better, for a triple-braided cord is not easily broken." You, your loved ones, and Jesus can make a strong cord that cannot be broken.

Acceptance

The final step in the grief process is acceptance. The point of acceptance can only be reached with hard work and by walking right through the middle of grief. It cannot be met by repressing pain, by ignoring it, or by sitting quietly and simply waiting for time to pass. It is not with the passage of time that acceptance is reached, but with the work that goes on during the passage of time.

I believe that just being aware of the grief process and wanting to get better will work in your favor. You may get discouraged periodically and feel that you are not making any progress. When this happens, talk to yourself tenderly. Remind yourself that grieving is hard work and takes time. It cannot be rushed. Be as gentle with yourself as you would be following open-heart surgery. Remember you have a broken heart and all wounds must be delicately nursed if they are to heal properly.

Do not be afraid to admit you are hurting and to ask for help. "I need a hug!" is a reasonable request.

During the grief process it is best to take only one day at a time. Do the best you can with each day and start fresh again in the morning. It is not necessary to look far ahead or make elaborate plans. Tell yourself, "I will not always feel this way"; then remind yourself you are getting better and that each day will get easier. If you hear these words often enough you will begin to believe them. Allow your tears to flow and look forward to the days ahead.

Scripture tells us to pray about everything and to pray incessantly. There is no better time to increase your prayer time than when you are grieving. Pray for help, for guidance, and for answers.

Bob Deits writes, "You can decide to grow through the most devastating loss in your life! A major part of the growing side of grief is coming to understand that, in the midst of a life-changing loss, we still have control over our own destiny. You may not be able to choose all of the circumstances of your life, but you can always choose your responses to anything that happens."[4] Pain is inevitable; suffering is optional.

Pain with a Purpose

When Linda's grandchild drowned in her backyard swimming pool, many loving friends came to comfort her. However, it was not until Sandy, whose young grandchild had also drowned, came that Linda felt help had truly arrived. They clung to each other and sobbed—two hearts entwined with a single agony binding them as one.

Once you are feeling strong again, you can reach out to other grievers, especially other grandparents, and comfort them. You can use the experience you have just come through to help others who are at the beginning of their personal road to recovery. You can walk beside them, hold their hands, and allow them to grab hold of you when they stumble over rocks in their paths.

When you help another you are allowing the pain you endured to serve a purpose instead of simply letting it be an empty time of suffering. It will not only help your fellow griever, but also complete your own healing.

The other day when I was mending a ripped seam, I stitched back and forth many more times than necessary in order to make sure it would be secure. When I turned the garment right side out to double-check, I smiled as I realized that the entire garment could fall apart, but this newly mended seam would last forever.

I believe hearts that have been ripped apart with grief can also be stitched and made whole again. And like a mended seam, a repaired heart will be twice as good, twice as sturdy, and never as easily torn again.

Take your heart, after it has been restored, and use it to help others.

Notes

Chapter 1

1. Fay Angus, *How to Do Everything Right and Live to Regret It* (San Diego: L. C. Enterprises, 1990), 158.

2. Dan Schaefer, *How Do We Tell the Children?* (New York: Newmarket Press, 1986), 3.

3. Quoted in Harold Blake Walker, *To Conquer Loneliness* (New York: Harper & Row, 1966), 142.

Chapter 2

1. Madeleine L'Engle, *Two Part Intervention: The Story of a Marriage* (San Francisco: Harper, 1989), 229.

2. C. S. Lewis, *A Grief Observed* (New York: Bantam Books, 1961), 1.

3. Bob Deits, *Life After Loss* (Tucson: Fisher Books, 1988), 15.

4. Larry Yeagley, *Grief Recovery* (self-published, 1981), 51, 55.

Chapter 3

1. Judy Tattlebaum, *The Courage to Grieve* (New York: Harper & Row, 1980), 93.

2. Ibid.

3. June Cerza Kolf, *Comfort and Care for the Critically Ill* (Grand Rapids: Baker, 1993), 161.

4. Bob Deits, *Life After Loss* (Tucson: Fisher Books, 1988), 98.

Suggested Reading

Children

Grollman, Earl A. *Explaining Death to Children.* Boston: Beacon Press, 1965. Practical information for dealing with children and death.

Kolf, June Cerza. *Teenagers Talk about Grief.* Grand Rapids: Baker Book House, 1990. Written exclusively for teenagers who have experienced loss from death.

Mellonie, Bryan and Robert Ingpen. *Lifetimes: The Beautiful Way to Explain Death to Children.* New York: Bantam Books, 1983. Written for the young child about life's beginnings and end for all living things.

Oyler, Chris. *Go toward the Light.* New York: Harper & Row, 1988. Insightful information by the mother of a seven-year-old who died of AIDS.

Schaefer, Dan and Christine Lyons. *How Do We Tell The Children?* New York: Newmarket Press, 1986. An honest step-by-step guide to help children understand death and grief.

Life After Death

Graham, Billy. *Facing Death and the Life After.* Waco: Word Books, 1987. Discusses death realistically with confidence that faith will conquer it.

Knapp, Ronald J. *Beyond Endurance: When a Child Dies.* New York: Schocken Books, 1986. Heartfelt information about the death of a child.

Moody, Raymond A. Jr., M.D. *Life After Life.* Carmel, NY: Guideposts, 1975. Case histories of people who have been clinically dead and survived to tell about their near death experiences.

————. *Reflections on Life After Life.* Boston: G. K. Hall, 1978. Follow-up and explanations of 1975 volume.

Perry, Paul. *The Light Beyond.* New York: Bantam Books, 1988. Case histories and information on the study of near death experiences, especially those of children.

Grief

Deits, Bob. *Life After Loss.* Tucson: Fisher Books, 1988. Practical steps for working through grief.

Grollman, Earl A. *When a Loved One Has Died.* Boston: Beacon Press, 1977. Easy to read, general information about death and the grief process.

Kolf, June Cerza. *How Can I Help?* Grand Rapids: Baker, 1989. Helpful information for appropriate actions when dealing with a bereaved person.

————. *When Will I Stop Hurting?* Grand Rapids: Baker, 1987. Addresses the emotions experienced following the loss of a loved one and offers help and hope for the future.

Lord, Janice Harris. *No Time for Goodbyes.* Ventura, Calif.: Pathway Publishing, 1991. Coping with sorrow, anger and injustice after a sudden, tragic death.

Schiff, Harriet. *The Bereaved Parent.* New York: Penguin Books. For insight into the grief process of parents.

Wright, H. Norman. *Beating the Blues.* Ventura, Calif.: Regal Books, 1988. A Christian approach to overcoming depression and stress.

Yeagley, Larry. *Grief Recovery.* Self-published, 1981. Can be ordered direct, from 1055 Horton Rd., Muskegon, MI 49445. Excellent information in easy-to-understand style.

Daily Journal